**LEVEL SEVEN**

# PIANO THEORY

T0088778

ISBN 978-1-4950-5731-1

**HAL•LEONARD®**

7777 W. BLUEMOUND RD. P.O. BOX 13819 MILWAUKEE, WI 53213

Visit Hal Leonard Online at
**www.halleonard.com**

Contact us:
**Hal Leonard**
7777 West Bluemound Road
Milwaukee, WI 53213
Email: info@halleonard.com

In Europe, contact:
**Hal Leonard Europe Limited**
42 Wigmore Street
Marylebone, London, W1U 2RN
Email: info@halleonardeurope.com

In Australia, contact:
**Hal Leonard Australia Pty. Ltd.**
4 Lentara Court
Cheltenham, Victoria, 3192 Australia
Email: info@halleonard.com.au

# To the Student

I wrote these books with you in mind. As a young student I often wondered how completing theory work-books would make me a better musician. The theory work often seemed separate from the music I was play-ing. My goal in *Essential Elements Piano Theory* is to provide you with the tools you will need to compose, improvise, play classical and popular music, or to better understand any other musical pursuit you might en-joy. In each "Musical Mastery" section of this book you will experience creative applications of the theory you have learned. The "Ear Training" pages will be completed with your teacher at the lesson. In this series you will begin to learn the building blocks of music, which make it possible for you to have fun at the piano. A practical understanding of theory enables you to see what is possible in music. I wish you all the best on your journey as you learn the language of music!

Sincerely,
Mona Rejino

# To the Teacher

I believe that knowledge of theory is most beneficial when a concept is followed directly by a musical application. In *Essential Elements Piano Theory*, learning theory becomes far more than completing worksheets. Students have the opportunity to see why learning a particular concept can help them become a better pianist right away. They can also see how the knowledge of musical patterns and chord progressions will enable them to be creative in their own musical pursuits: composing, arrang-ing, improvising, playing classical and popular music, accompanying, or any other.

A free download of the *Teacher's Answer Key* is available at www.halleonard.com/eeptheory7answer.

# Acknowledgements

I would like to thank Hal Leonard LLC for providing me the opportunity to put these theoretical thoughts down on paper and share them with others. I owe a debt of gratitude to Jennifer Linn, who has helped with this project every step of the way. These books would not have been possible with-out the support of my family: To my husband, Richard, for his wisdom and amazing ability to solve dilemmas; to my children, Maggie and Adam, for helping me think outside the box.

# TABLE OF CONTENTS

# UNIT 1

## REVIEW

1. Add bar lines to complete this rhythmic pattern.

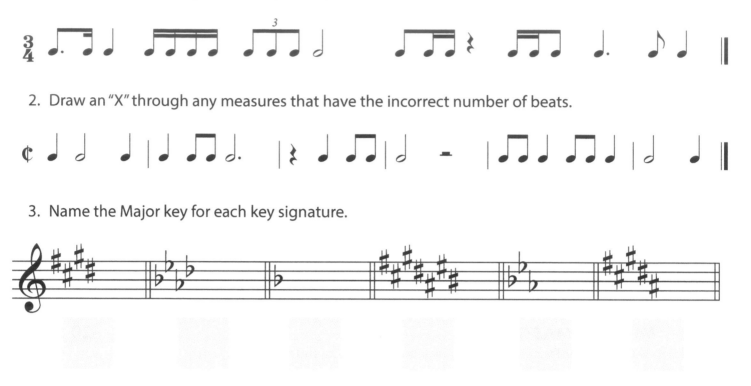

2. Draw an "X" through any measures that have the incorrect number of beats.

3. Name the Major key for each key signature.

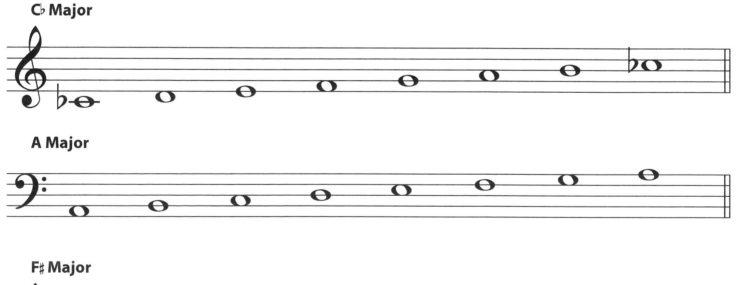

4. Add the sharps or flats needed to complete each scale.

**D♭ Major**

**C♭ Major**

**A Major**

**F♯ Major**

5. Draw a note above the given note to form these harmonic intervals. Add accidentals as needed.

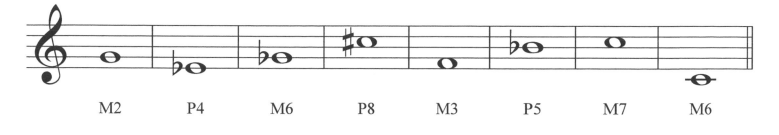

M2    P4    M6    P8    M3    P5    M7    M6

6. Write the letter name of each triad and indicate whether it is Major (**Chord letter**), minor (**m**), Augmented (**+**) or diminished ( **°** ).

7. Draw the following root position triads.

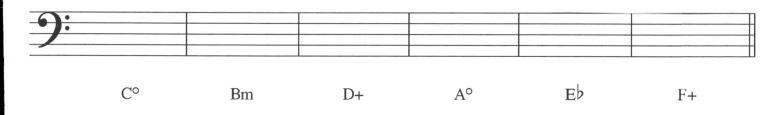

C°          Bm          D+          A°          E♭          F+

8. Circle the correct name for each cadence in the given key.

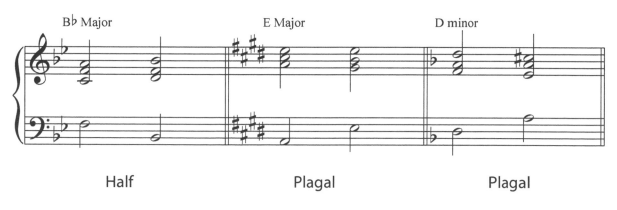

Half                Plagal              Plagal

Authentic           Authentic           Half

5

9. Following the musical example, write the chord progression in the keys given. Each chord will share one common tone.

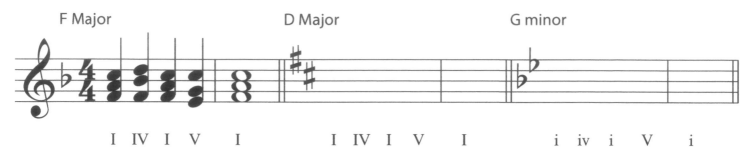

F Major                      D Major                      G minor

I   IV   I   V    I           I   IV   I   V    I           i   iv   i   V    i

10. Draw these root position dominant seventh chords, adding the correct accidentals. *The dominant seventh chord in root position consists of a Major triad plus a minor third. The first one is done for you.*

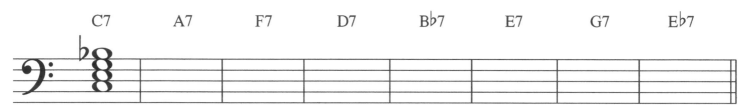

C7       A7       F7       D7       B♭7       E7       G7       E♭7

11. Draw the dominant seventh (V7) chord in root position. Start on the dominant note in each key.

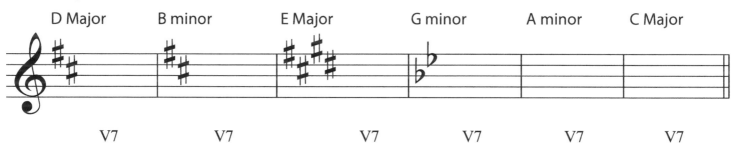

D Major       B minor       E Major       G minor       A minor       C Major

V7           V7           V7           V7           V7           V7

12. Complete each chord progression by adding the missing chord.
     a. Draw I or i chords in root position.
     b. Draw IV or iv chords in 2nd inversion.
     c. Draw V7 chords in 1st inversion, omitting the 5th.

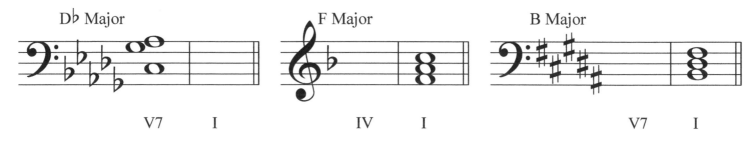

D♭ Major               F Major               B Major

     V7     I             IV     I             V7     I

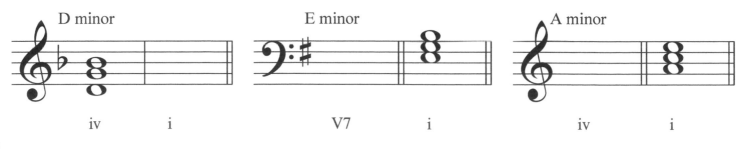

D minor               E minor               A minor

     iv     i             V7     i             iv     i

# Time Signatures and Rhythm

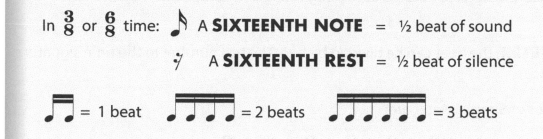

In $\frac{3}{8}$ or $\frac{6}{8}$ time: ♪ A **SIXTEENTH NOTE** = ½ beat of sound

♪ A **SIXTEENTH REST** = ½ beat of silence

♫ = 1 beat   ♫♫ = 2 beats   ♫♫♫ = 3 beats

1. Clap and count these rhythms.

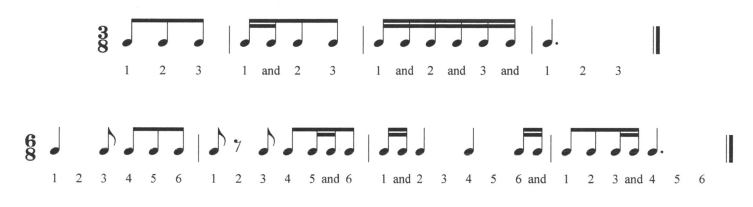

2. Write the counts below each measure, using a + sign for the word "and." Clap and count the rhythms.

3. Add bar lines. Write the counts below each measure. Choose one key on the piano and play the rhythm while counting aloud.

The **METER** of music is its rhythmic structure. Meter organizes stressed and unstressed beats into measures. Meter is notated at the beginning of a composition by the time signature.

In **SIMPLE METER**, the beat can be divided by two. The top number in the time signature will be 2, 3 or 4.

Examples of Simple Meter are:

$$\frac{2}{2} \quad \frac{3}{2} \quad \frac{2}{4} \quad \frac{3}{4} \quad \frac{4}{4} \quad \frac{3}{8}$$

In **COMPOUND METER**, the beat can be divided by three. The top number in the time signature will be 6, 9 or 12.

Examples of Compound Meter are:

$$\frac{6}{4} \quad \frac{9}{4} \quad \frac{6}{8} \quad \frac{9}{8} \quad \frac{12}{8}$$

In **ASYMMETRICAL METER**, the measure cannot be divided into equal parts which causes the pulse to feel irregular. Asymmetrical Meter is the combination of two simple meters.

Examples of Asymmetrical Meter are:

$$\frac{5}{4} \quad \frac{7}{4} \quad \frac{5}{8} \quad \frac{7}{8}$$

4. Complete each time signature by adding the top number in the box.

    Simple              Compound            Asymmetrical          Compound

5. Circle the correct meter for each time signature given.

a. **3/8**  simple
compound
asymmetrical

b. **7/4**  simple
compound
asymmetrical

c. **9/8**  simple
compound
asymmetrical

d. **5/4**  simple
compound
asymmetrical

e. **12/8**  simple
compound
asymmetrical

f. **2/4**  simple
compound
asymmetrical

6. Each measure is characteristic of a particular meter. Fill in each box with the correct time signature. Choose from **2/4  3/4  4/4  5/4  7/4  3/8  6/8  9/8**

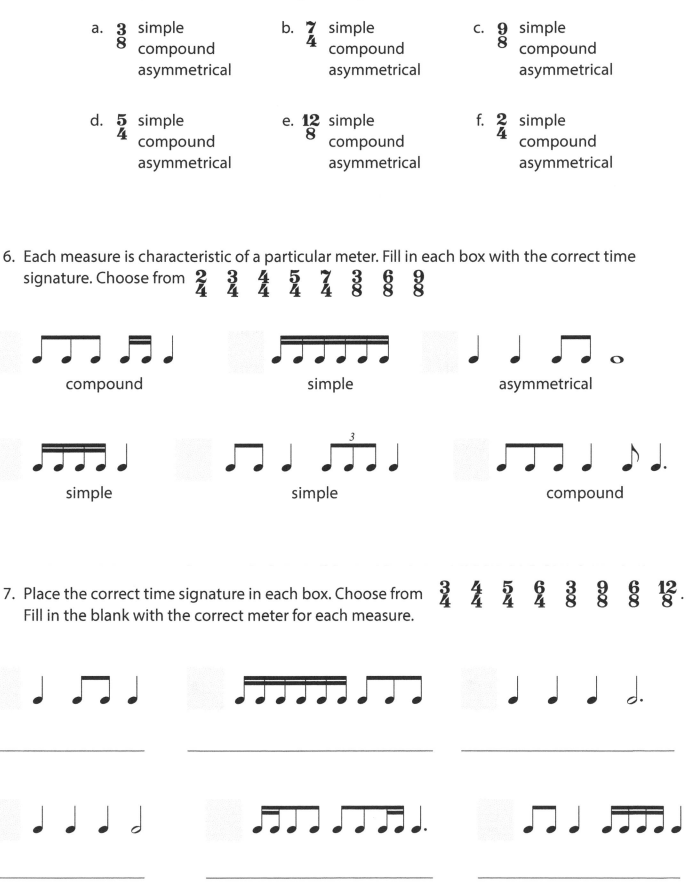

compound

simple

asymmetrical

simple

simple

compound

7. Place the correct time signature in each box. Choose from **3/4  4/4  5/4  6/4  3/8  9/8  6/8  12/8** .
Fill in the blank with the correct meter for each measure.

_____

_____

_____

_____

_____

_____

## Minor Sharp Key Signatures and Scales

Keys are related by Perfect 5ths. Begin with the key of a minor (no sharps or flats) and go up a 5th to the key of e minor (one sharp.) Go up a 5th from e minor to the key of b minor (two sharps.) The pattern continues through all the sharp keys.

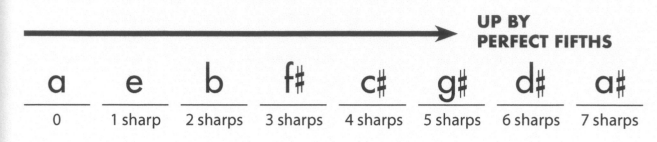

**UP BY PERFECT FIFTHS**

| a | e | b | f♯ | c♯ | g♯ | d♯ | a♯ |
|---|---|---|----|----|----|----|----|
| 0 | 1 sharp | 2 sharps | 3 sharps | 4 sharps | 5 sharps | 6 sharps | 7 sharps |

1. Fill in the blanks with the correct letters (lower case) and numbers.

    a. A 5th above **a** is the key of _____ which has _____ sharp.

    b. A 5th above **e** is the key of _____ which has _____ sharps.

    c. A 5th above **b** is the key of _____ which has _____ sharps.

    d. A 5th above **f♯** is the key of _____ which has _____ sharps.

    e. A 5th above **c♯** is the key of _____ which has _____ sharps.

    f. A 5th above **g♯** is the key of _____ which has _____ sharps.

    g. A 5th above **d♯** is the key of _____ which has _____ sharps.

2. Write the name of the minor key signature in each box. *The first one is done for you.*

a minor

3. Write the name of each Major key signature in the first blank. Write the name of each relative minor key signature in the second blank. *To find the relative minor key, count down three half steps from the Major key. The first one is done for you.*

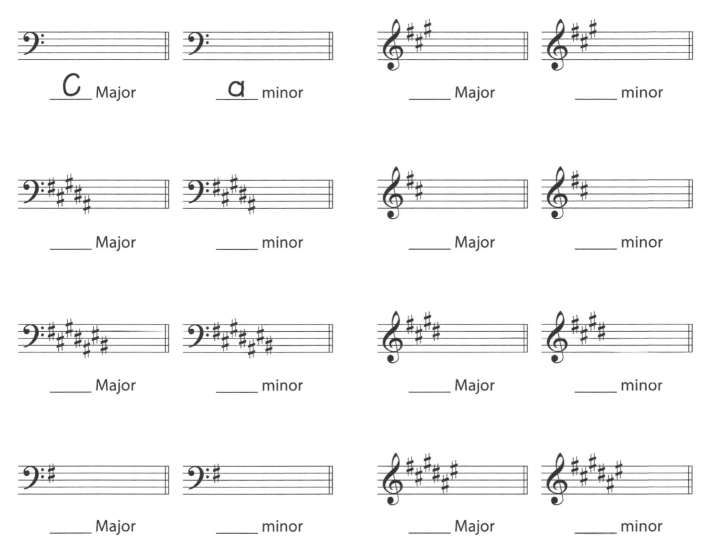

_C_ Major          _a_ minor          _____ Major          _____ minor

_____ Major          _____ minor          _____ Major          _____ minor

_____ Major          _____ minor          _____ Major          _____ minor

_____ Major          _____ minor          _____ Major          _____ minor

4. Draw the minor key signature named below each measure.

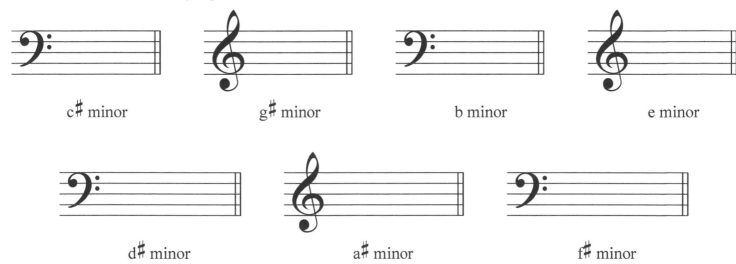

c# minor          g# minor          b minor          e minor

d# minor          a# minor          f# minor

5. Write the following Major and relative minor scales ascending. *The first note is given.*

6. Draw a line connecting each form of minor scale to its definition.

| Harmonic | It follows the key signature with no changes. |
| Natural | The sixth and seventh notes are raised a half step ascending, and are lowered descending. |
| Melodic | The seventh note is raised a half step ascending and descending. |

7. Add accidentals to complete the following scales.

c# Harmonic Minor

c# Melodic Minor

f# Harmonic Minor

f# Melodic Minor

# Minor Flat Key Signatures and Scales

Begin with the key of a minor and go down a Perfect 5th to the key of d minor (one flat.) Go down a 5th from d minor to the key of g minor (two flats.) The pattern continues through all the flat keys.

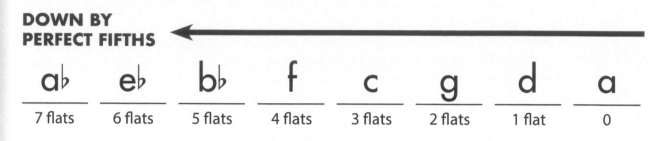

1. Fill in the blanks with the correct letters and numbers.

   a. A 5th below **a** is the key of _____ which has _____ flat.

   b. A 5th below **d** is the key of _____ which has _____ flats.

   c. A 5th below **g** is the key of _____ which has _____ flats.

   d. A 5th below **c** is the key of _____ which has _____ flats.

   e. A 5th below **f** is the key of _____ which has _____ flats.

   f. A 5th below **b♭** is the key of _____ which has _____ flats.

   g. A 5th below **e♭** is the key of _____ which has _____ flats.

2. Write the name of the minor key signature in each box.

3. Write the name of each Major key signature in the first blank. Write the name of each relative minor key signature in the second blank.

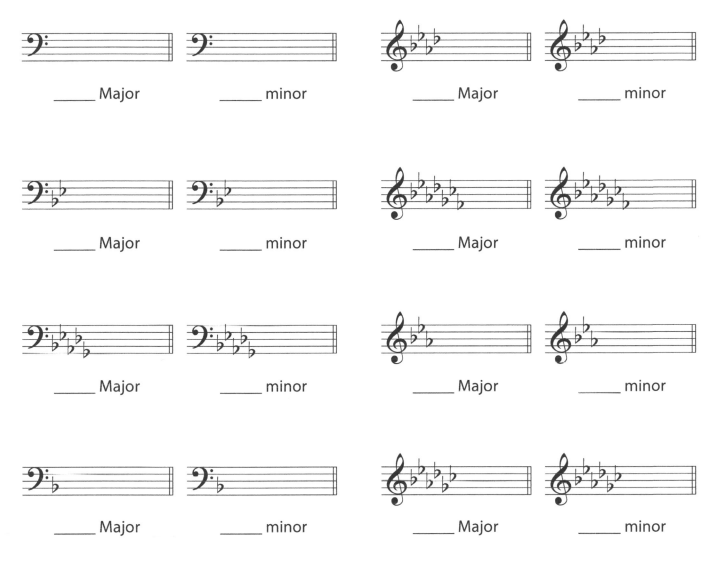

\_\_\_\_\_ Major    \_\_\_\_\_ minor          \_\_\_\_\_ Major    \_\_\_\_\_ minor

\_\_\_\_\_ Major    \_\_\_\_\_ minor          \_\_\_\_\_ Major    \_\_\_\_\_ minor

\_\_\_\_\_ Major    \_\_\_\_\_ minor          \_\_\_\_\_ Major    \_\_\_\_\_ minor

\_\_\_\_\_ Major    \_\_\_\_\_ minor          \_\_\_\_\_ Major    \_\_\_\_\_ minor

4. Draw the minor key signature named below each measure.

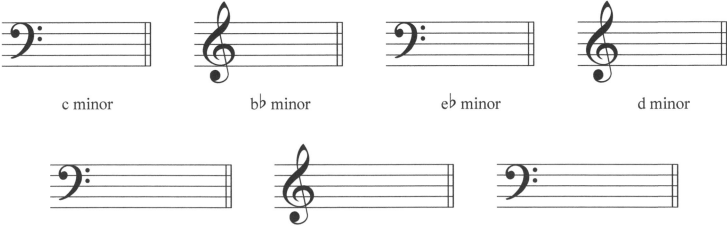

c minor          b♭ minor          e♭ minor          d minor

f minor          g minor          a♭ minor

15

5. Write the following Major and relative minor scales ascending. *The first note is given.*

Ab Major Scale

f Natural Minor Scale

Cb Major Scale

ab Natural Minor Scale

Db Major Scale

bb Natural Minor Scale

Eb Major Scale

c Natural Minor Scale

Gb Major Scale

eb Natural Minor Scale

Bb Major Scale

g Natural Minor Scale

F Major Scale

d Natural Minor Scale

6. Add accidentals to complete the following scales.

c Harmonic Minor

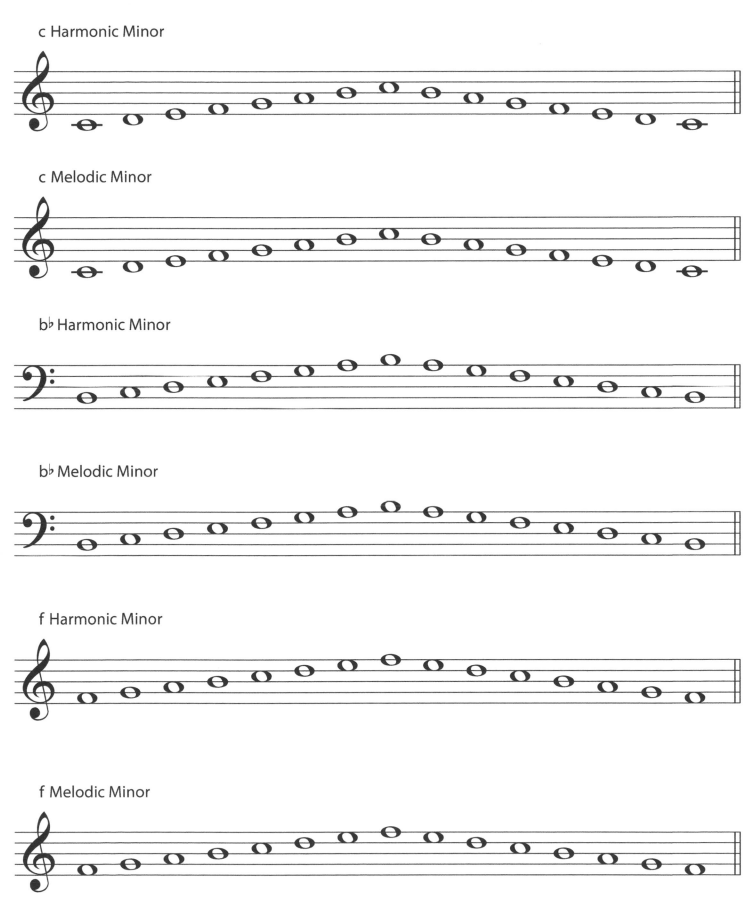

c Melodic Minor

b♭ Harmonic Minor

b♭ Melodic Minor

f Harmonic Minor

f Melodic Minor

## Minor Circle of Fifths

The **CIRCLE OF FIFTHS** is a diagram showing the relationship between key signatures.

The keys are arranged a Perfect 5th apart. Moving clockwise from the key of a minor at the top, each key signature adds one sharp. Moving counterclockwise from the key of a minor, each key signature adds one flat.

The keys at the bottom are enharmonic keys. They sound the same, but are written and named differently.

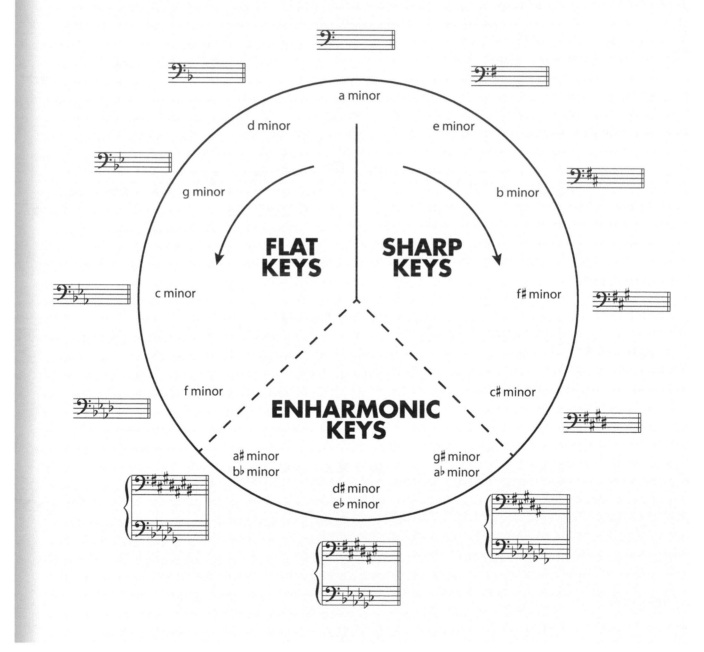

1. Name the order of sharps.

_____ _____ _____ _____ _____ _____ _____

2. Name the order of flats.

_____ _____ _____ _____ _____ _____ _____

3. Complete the Circle of Fifths by drawing the correct key signature on each treble staff below.

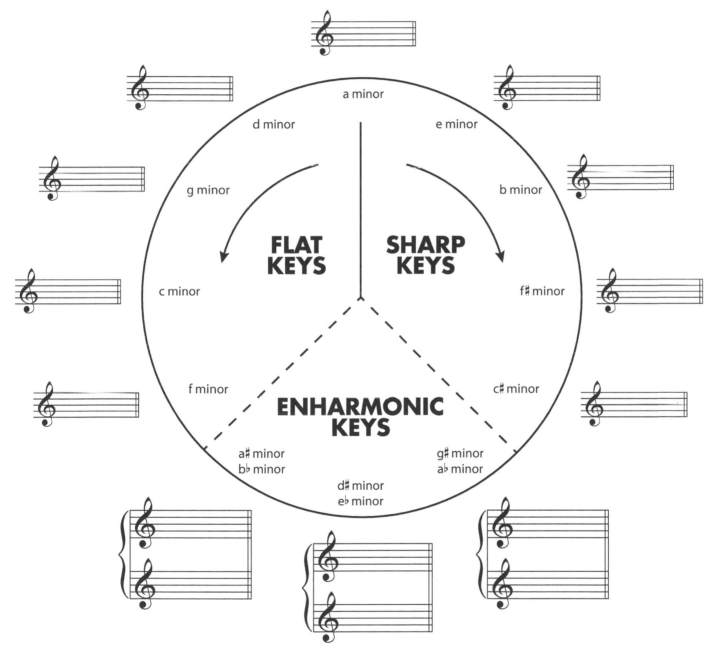

# MUSICAL MASTERY

## Ear Training

1. You will hear one rhythm from each pair. Circle the rhythm you hear.

2. You will hear the following intervals played in broken and blocked form: M2, P4, P5, M6 and P8. Name the interval by type and size in each blank.

    1. _____    2. _____    3. _____    4. _____    5. _____    6. _____

3. You will hear four scales ascending and descending. Circle the type of scale that you hear.

    a.   Major     natural minor     harmonic minor     melodic minor

    b.   Major     natural minor     harmonic minor     melodic minor

    c.   Major     natural minor     harmonic minor     melodic minor

    d.   Major     natural minor     harmonic minor     melodic minor

# Reading Mastery: Playing Around the Circle of Fifths

1. Complete the linear Circle of Fifths by filling in the blanks.

Down by Perfect 5ths ⟵⟶ Up by Perfect 5ths

a

___  ___  ___  ___  ___  ___  __a__  ___  ___  ___  ___  ___  ___  ___

2. Play around the Circle of Fifths through all of the minor keys. *The left hand bass line follows the Circle of Fifths.*

# Rhythm Mastery

1. Complete the time signature by adding the top number in each shaded box.

2. Fill in the blank with the correct meter: Simple, Compound or Asymmetrical.

a. *Sonatina Op. 36, No. 2 (III)* by Clementi

_____

b. *Sonntag (Sunday) Op. 101, No. 18* by Gurlitt

_____

c. *Bulgarian Rhythm* by Bartok

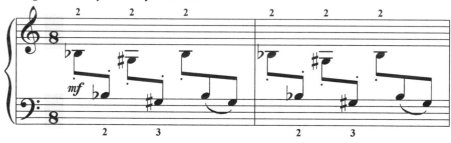

_____

d. *Gavotte in A Minor* by Pachelbel

_____

e. *Quiet Morning* by Maykapar

_____

# Double Sharps and Double Flats

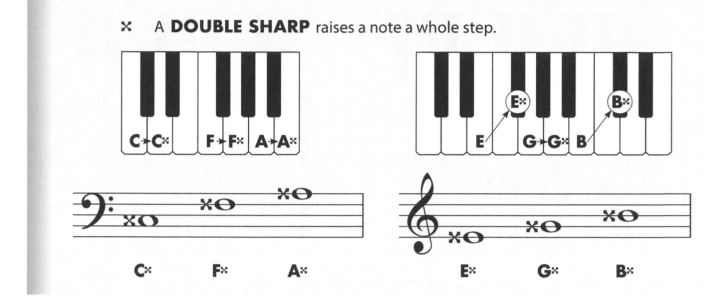

×   A **DOUBLE SHARP** raises a note a whole step.

1. Write an enharmonic name for each of the following notes using double sharps. *The first one is done for you.*

    G = __Fx__      E = _____      C♯ = _____      A = _____      F♯ = _____

2. Using accidentals, raise each note a whole step from the given note. Do not change the letter name. *The first one is done for you.*

3. Using accidentals, lower each note a whole step from the given note. Do not change the letter name. *The first one is done for you.*

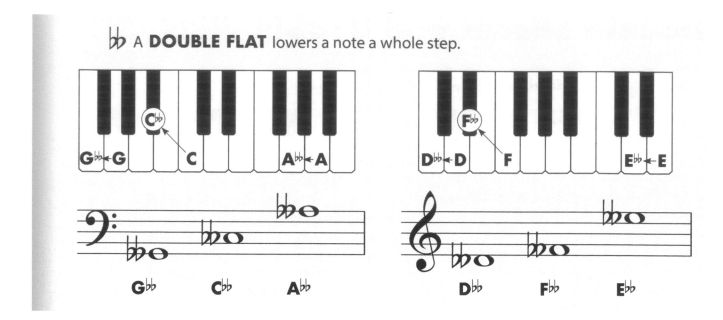

**♭♭ A DOUBLE FLAT** lowers a note a whole step.

4. Write an enharmonic name for each of the following notes using double flats. *The first one is done for you.*

G = **A♭♭**    D = _____    A = _____    B♭ = _____    F = _____

5. Using accidentals, raise each note a whole step from the given note. Do not change the letter name. *The first one is done for you.*

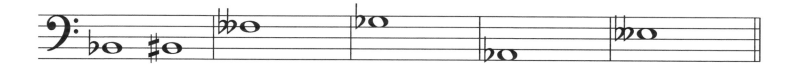

6. Using accidentals, lower each note a whole step from the given note. Do not change the letter name. *The first one is done for you.*

# Major and Minor Intervals

When the tonic and upper note of an interval belong to the same major scale, it is called a **diatonic interval**.

Key of F Major

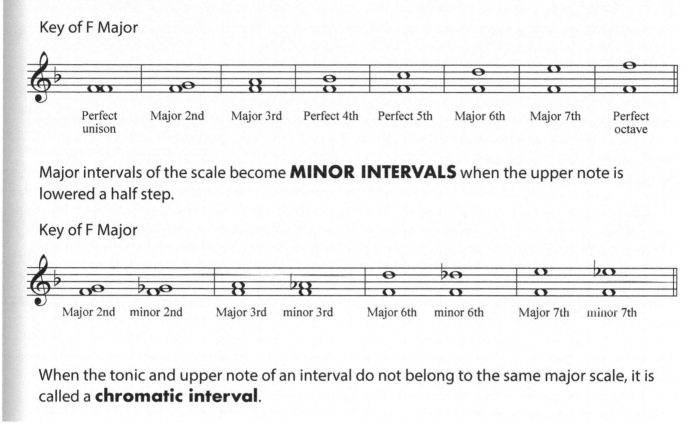

| Perfect unison | Major 2nd | Major 3rd | Perfect 4th | Perfect 5th | Major 6th | Major 7th | Perfect octave |

Major intervals of the scale become **MINOR INTERVALS** when the upper note is lowered a half step.

Key of F Major

| Major 2nd | minor 2nd | Major 3rd | minor 3rd | Major 6th | minor 6th | Major 7th | minor 7th |

When the tonic and upper note of an interval do not belong to the same major scale, it is called a **chromatic interval**.

1. Draw the minor interval after each Major interval. *Notice the key signature and use accidentals as needed.*

Key of G Major

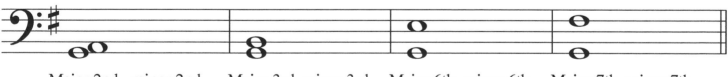

| Major 2nd | minor 2nd | Major 3rd | minor 3rd | Major 6th | minor 6th | Major 7th | minor 7th |

Key of Eb Major

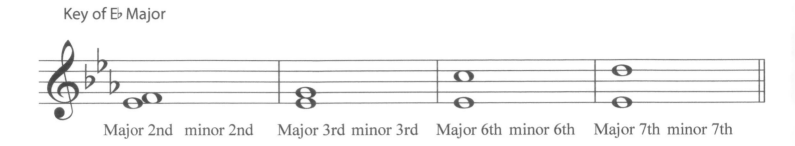

Major 2nd   minor 2nd      Major 3rd  minor 3rd    Major 6th  minor 6th    Major 7th  minor 7th

2. Name the following intervals. Use **M** for Major and **m** for minor. *The first one is done for you.*

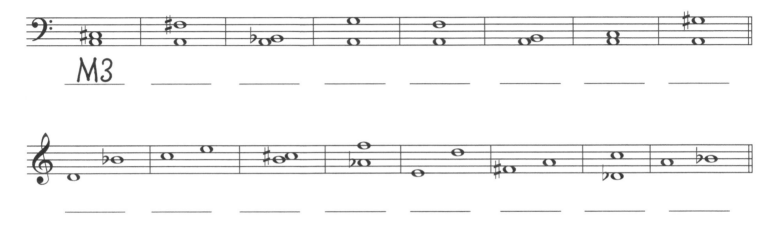

M3

3. Draw a note above the given note to complete the harmonic intervals. Add accidentals as needed.

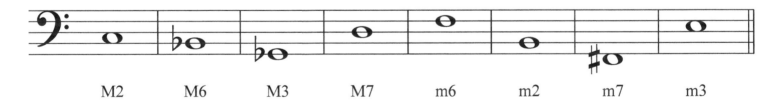

M2          M6          M3          M7          m6          m2          m7          m3

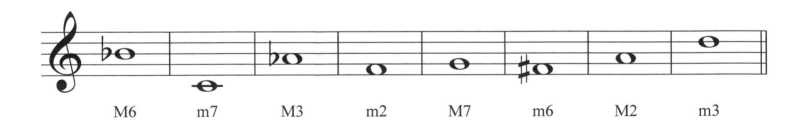

M6          m7          M3          m2          M7          m6          M2          m3

# Augmented and Diminished Intervals

Perfect and Major intervals of the scale become **AUGMENTED INTERVALS** when the upper note is raised a half step.

A DOUBLE SHARP raises a sharp note a half step.

**Key of G Major**

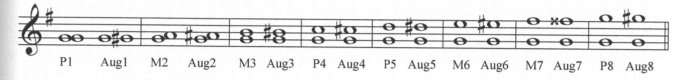

| P1 | Aug1 | M2 | Aug2 | M3 | Aug3 | P4 | Aug4 | P5 | Aug5 | M6 | Aug6 | M7 | Aug7 | P8 | Aug8 |

Perfect and minor intervals of the scale become **DIMINISHED INTERVALS** when the upper note is lowered a half step.

A DOUBLE FLAT lowers a flat note a half step.

**Key of G Major**

| m2 | dim2 | m3 | dim3 | P4 | dim4 | P5 | dim5 | m6 | dim6 | m7 | dim7 | P8 | dim8 |

1. Name the following Augmented intervals. Use **Aug** for Augmented. *The first one is done for you.*

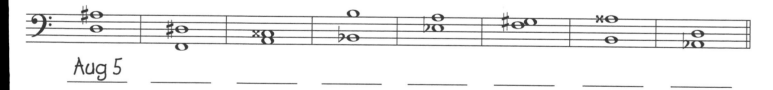

Aug 5 _____ _____ _____ _____ _____ _____ _____

2. Draw a note above the given note to complete the Augmented harmonic intervals.

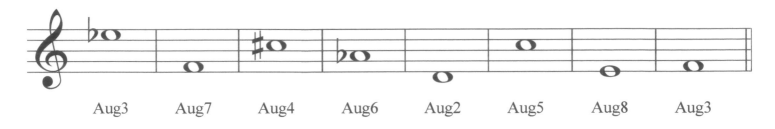

Aug3     Aug7     Aug4     Aug6     Aug2     Aug5     Aug8     Aug3

3. Name the following diminished intervals. Use **dim** for diminished. *The first one is done for you.*

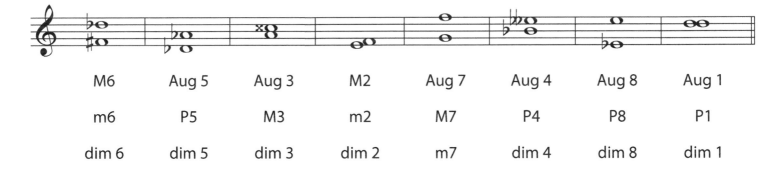

dim 4

4. Circle the correct answer for each interval.

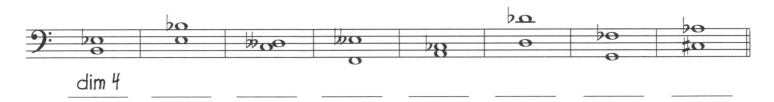

| M6 | Aug 5 | Aug 3 | M2 | Aug 7 | Aug 4 | Aug 8 | Aug 1 |
|----|-------|-------|----|-------|-------|-------|-------|
| m6 | P5 | M3 | m2 | M7 | P4 | P8 | P1 |
| dim 6 | dim 5 | dim 3 | dim 2 | m7 | dim 4 | dim 8 | dim 1 |

5. Identify each interval by type (P, M, m, Aug or dim) and size. *The first one is done for you.*

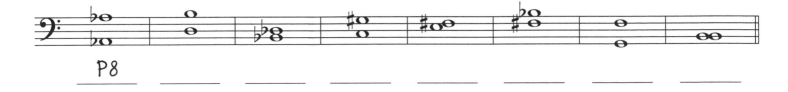

P8

# Phrases and Motives

A **PHRASE** is a musical thought or idea. Phrases may be thought of as musical sentences.

A melody often has two parts:

A **Question** phrase ends on a note other than tonic.
An **Answer** phrase ends on the tonic note.

*Tarantella Op. 157*, No. 1 by Spindler

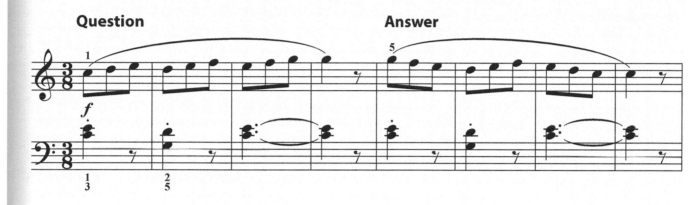

1. What is the key signature for the musical excerpt below? _____

2. Identify the question and answer phrases by filling in the blanks.

*Russian Folk Song* by Beethoven

A **MOTIVE (motif)** is a short melodic or rhythmic pattern that is used repeatedly throughout a piece. **REPETITION** occurs when a motive is repeated.

*Musette* from *Notebook for Anna Magdalena Bach*

3. Identify the motive and its repetition by filling in the blanks.

*Little Bird Op. 117, No. 7* by Gurlitt

**SEQUENCE** is the repeating of a melodic pattern or motive at a higher or lower pitch.

*Giga* by Arnold

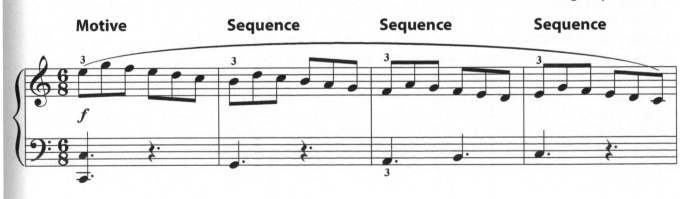

4. Identify the motive and sequences by filling in the blanks below.

*Scherzo Op. 39, No. 12* by Kabalevsky

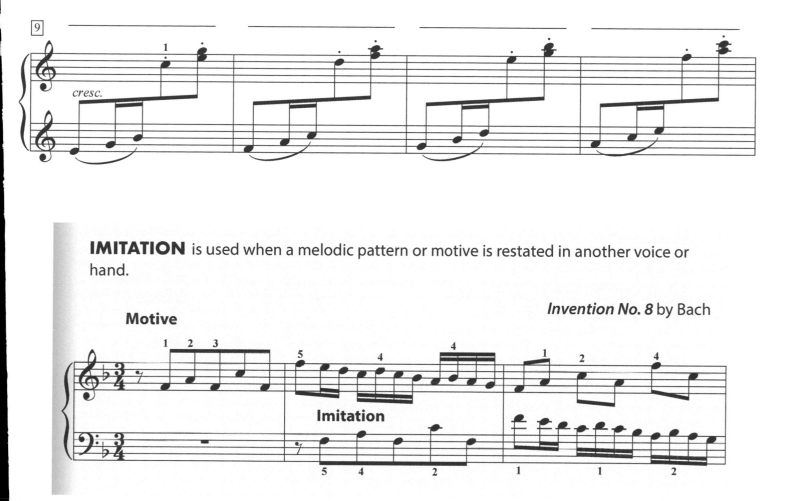

**IMITATION** is used when a melodic pattern or motive is restated in another voice or hand.

*Invention No. 8* by Bach

**Motive**

**Imitation**

5. Label the motive and imitation in the following excerpt.

*Invention No. 4* by Bach

# MUSICAL MASTERY

## Ear Training

1. You will hear four measures of rhythmic dictation. Fill in the blank measures with the rhythm you hear.

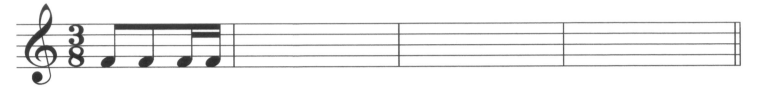

2. The first melody in each pair is Major. The second melody is minor. Circle the one you hear.

3. You will hear melodic patterns using repetition or sequence. Circle the one you hear.

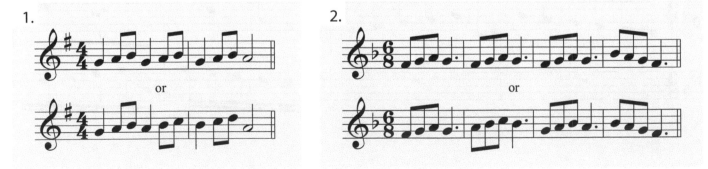

# TERM QUIZ

1. Mark each statement as either true or false.

   _____ a. A double flat raises a note a whole step.

   _____ b. A double sharp raises a sharp note a half step.

   _____ c. To change a Major interval to minor, lower the upper note a half step.

   _____ d. Perfect and minor intervals of the scale become Augmented intervals
   when the upper note is lowered a half step.

   _____ e. The key signatures of both A♭ Major and f minor contain four flats.

   _____ f. The key signatures of both E Major and f♯ minor contain three sharps.

2. Choose the correct word to complete each sentence, then fill in the blank.

   a. When the tonic and upper note of an interval belong to the same Major scale, it is
   called a _____ interval.

        chromatic     diatonic     diminished

   b. When the tonic and upper note of an interval do not belong to the same Major scale it
   is called a _____ interval.

        chromatic     diatonic     natural

   c. The meter of music is its _____ structure.

        harmonic     melodic     rhythmic

   d. The time signature $\frac{3}{4}$ is an example of _____ meter.

        simple     compound     asymmetrical

   e. _____ is the repeating of a melodic pattern at a higher or lower pitch.

        repetition     sequence     imitation

   f. A _____ is a short melodic or rhythmic pattern that is used repeatedly
   throughout a piece.

        motive     phrase     repetition

# Composing Mastery

1. Compose an answer phrase for each question phrase. *Your answer should end on the tonic note.*

2. Continue the one-measure motive as a sequence. Begin each measure on the given note.

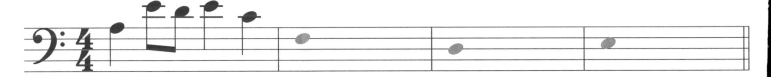

3. Beginning on the given note, write an imitation of the two-measure pattern in the bass staff.

4. Play all of the melodies above.

# Musical Signs and Terms

An asterisk (*) indicates words that are new to this book.

The following terms help describe the mood or style of the music.

| Italian Name | Meaning |
|---|---|
| cantabile | in a singing style |
| leggiero | lightly |
| scherzando | playful |
| senza | without |
| loco | play as written |
| giocoso* | joyfully, humorous |
| spiritoso* | spirited |
| marcato* | marked, emphasized |
| animato* | animated, lively |
| morendo* | dying; fading away |
| sostenuto* | sustained |
| simile* | continue in a similar manner |
| tranquillo* | calm, tranquil |

1. Write the definition for each term in the blanks.

animato _____     leggiero _____

morendo _____     senza _____

tranquillo _____     cantabile _____

giocoso _____     sostenuto _____

scherzando _____     marcato _____

loco _____     spiritoso _____

simile _____

**ARTICULATION** signs tell how to play and release the keys.

| Name | Sign (Symbol) | Meaning |
|------|---------------|---------|
| martellato | | short and accented |
| portato* | | halfway between staccato and legato |

**TEMPO** marks tell what speed to play the music.

## Italian Name   Meaning

| Italian Name | Meaning |
|--------------|---------|
| lento | slow; slower than *adagio* |
| vivo | lively, bright |
| grave | slow, solemn |
| stringendo* | hurrying the tempo; increasing the tension |
| ritenuto* | held back; immediately slower |

1. Write the definition for each Italian tempo mark.

vivo _____     lento _____

stringendo _____

grave _____     ritenuto _____

# Other Musical Symbols

*15ma*    **Quindicesima** means to play two octaves higher, or lower, than written.

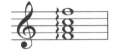    **Arpeggio**   A chord whose pitches are played in succession; harp-like

♪    **Grace Note***   An ornamental note played quickly, before the beat

*t.c.*    **Tre Corde***   Release the soft (left) pedal.

*u.c.*    **Una Corde***   Depress the soft (left) pedal.

# REVIEW

1. Match each term or symbol with its definition by writing the correct letter in the blank.

| | | |
|---|---|---|
| _____ simile | | a. joyfully, humorous |
| _____ giocoso | | b. animated, lively |
| _____ *u.c.* | | c. spirited |
| _____ stringendo | | d. an ornamental note played quickly, before the beat |
| _____ animato | | e. dying, fading away |
| _____ portato | | f. continue in a similar manner |
| _____ morendo | | g. double sharp |
| _____ ♪ | | h. depress the soft (left) pedal |
| _____ sostenuto | | i. halfway between *staccato* and *legato* |
| _____ 𝄪 | | j. double flat |
| _____ marcato | | k. held back, immediately slower |
| _____ spiritoso | | l. sustained |
| _____ tranquillo | | m. release the soft (left) pedal |
| _____ *t.c.* | | n. hurrying the tempo; increasing the tension |
| _____ ritenuto | | o. marked, emphasized |
| _____ ♭♭ | | p. calm, tranquil |

2. Add all the notes and rests as you would count them in **6/8** time. Write the total number of beats in the box.

3. Fill in the blanks with the correct answer.

    a. In _____ meter, the top number in the time signature will be 2, 3 or 4.

    b. In _____ meter, the top number in the time signature will be 6, 9 or 12.

    c. In _____ meter, the top number in the time signature will be 5 or 7.

4. Complete the linear Circle of Fifths for minor keys.

Down by Perfect 5ths ⬅———————    ———————➡ Up by Perfect 5ths

    **a**

____ ____ ____ ____ ____ ____ ____ ____ ____ ____ ____ ____

5. Write the lower case letter name in the blanks for these minor key signatures.

6. Name each Major key signature and its relative minor key signature.

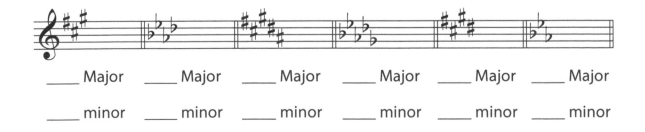

____ Major    ____ Major    ____ Major    ____ Major    ____ Major    ____ Major

____ minor    ____ minor    ____ minor    ____ minor    ____ minor    ____ minor

7. Circle the correct name for each scale.

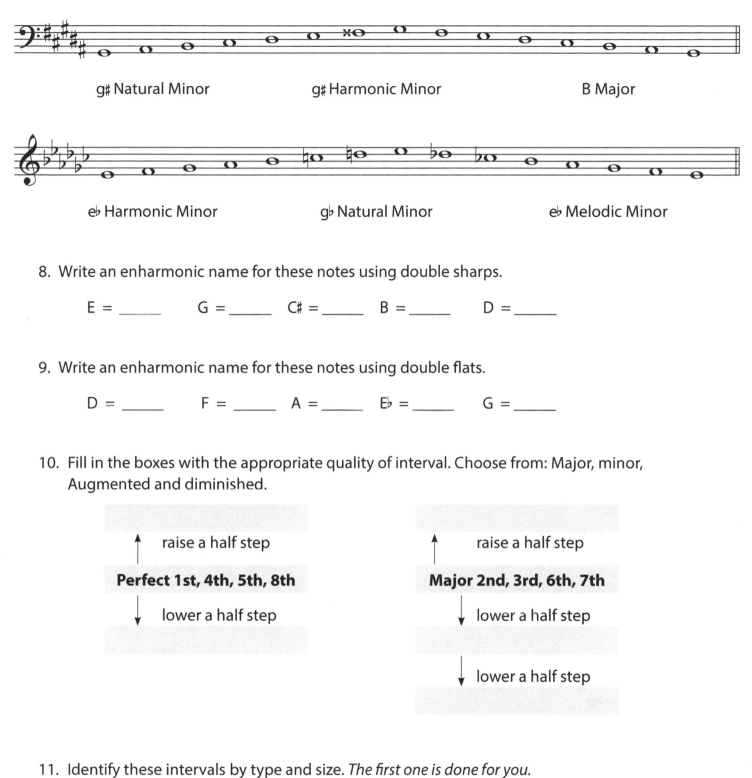

g♯ Natural Minor          g♯ Harmonic Minor          B Major

e♭ Harmonic Minor          g♭ Natural Minor          e♭ Melodic Minor

8. Write an enharmonic name for these notes using double sharps.

   E = _____     G = _____     C♯ = _____     B = _____     D = _____

9. Write an enharmonic name for these notes using double flats.

   D = _____     F = _____     A = _____     E♭ = _____     G = _____

10. Fill in the boxes with the appropriate quality of interval. Choose from: Major, minor, Augmented and diminished.

|  | raise a half step |  |  | raise a half step |
| **Perfect 1st, 4th, 5th, 8th** | | | **Major 2nd, 3rd, 6th, 7th** | |
|  | lower a half step |  |  | lower a half step |
|  |  |  |  | lower a half step |

11. Identify these intervals by type and size. *The first one is done for you.*

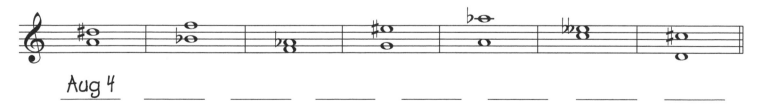

Aug 4   _____   _____   _____   _____   _____   _____   _____

12. Study the musical excerpts below. Fill in the blanks with the correct answer.

*Polonaise in G minor* from *Notebook for Anna Magdalena Bach*

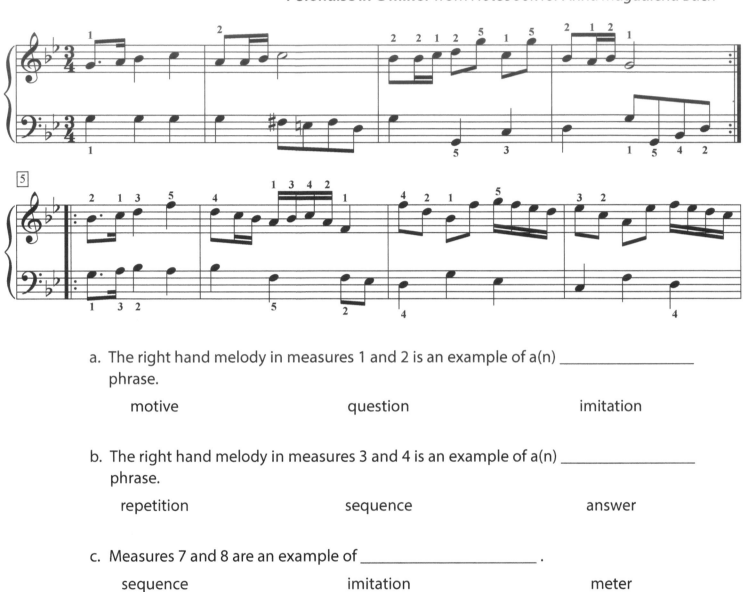

a.  The right hand melody in measures 1 and 2 is an example of a(n) _____ phrase.

    motive                              question                          imitation

b.  The right hand melody in measures 3 and 4 is an example of a(n) _____ phrase.

    repetition                         sequence                      answer

c.  Measures 7 and 8 are an example of _____ .

    sequence                         imitation                      meter

*Menuet in A Minor* by Bach

a.  The left hand melody in measures 1 – 4 is an example of _____ .

    answer                             imitation                       sequence

# MUSICAL MASTERY

## Ear Training

1. You will hear eight measures of melodic dictation. Fill in the blank measures with the notes and rhythms you hear. *The last note in measure 4 will end on the dominant, and measure 8 will end on the tonic.*

2. You will hear one interval from each pair. Circle the interval you hear.

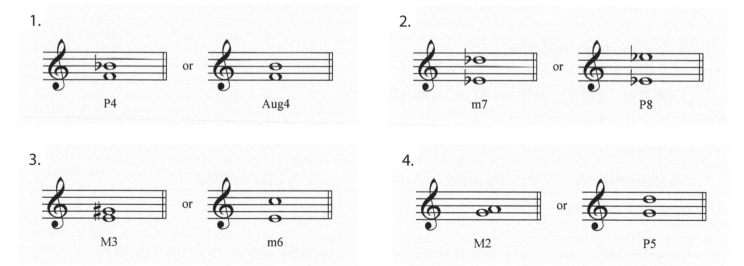

3. You will hear six triads played in broken and blocked form. Identify them as Major, minor, Augmented or diminished.

# Analysis

Study this excerpt from "Study in A Minor," then answer the questions about it.

# Study in A Minor
Op. 47, No. 3

Stephen Heller
(1813–1888)

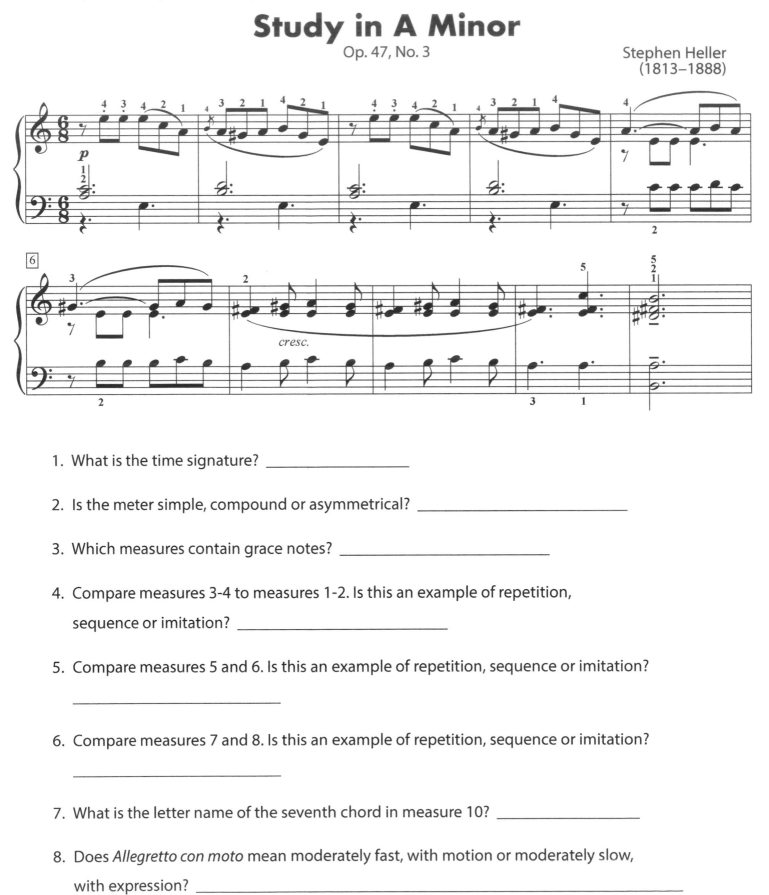

1. What is the time signature? _____

2. Is the meter simple, compound or asymmetrical? _____

3. Which measures contain grace notes? _____

4. Compare measures 3-4 to measures 1-2. Is this an example of repetition, sequence or imitation? _____

5. Compare measures 5 and 6. Is this an example of repetition, sequence or imitation? _____

6. Compare measures 7 and 8. Is this an example of repetition, sequence or imitation? _____

7. What is the letter name of the seventh chord in measure 10? _____

8. Does *Allegretto con moto* mean moderately fast, with motion or moderately slow, with expression? _____

Study this excerpt from "Sonatina in E Minor," then answer the questions about it.

# Sonatina
## Op. 157, No. 8

Fritz Spindler
(1817–1905)

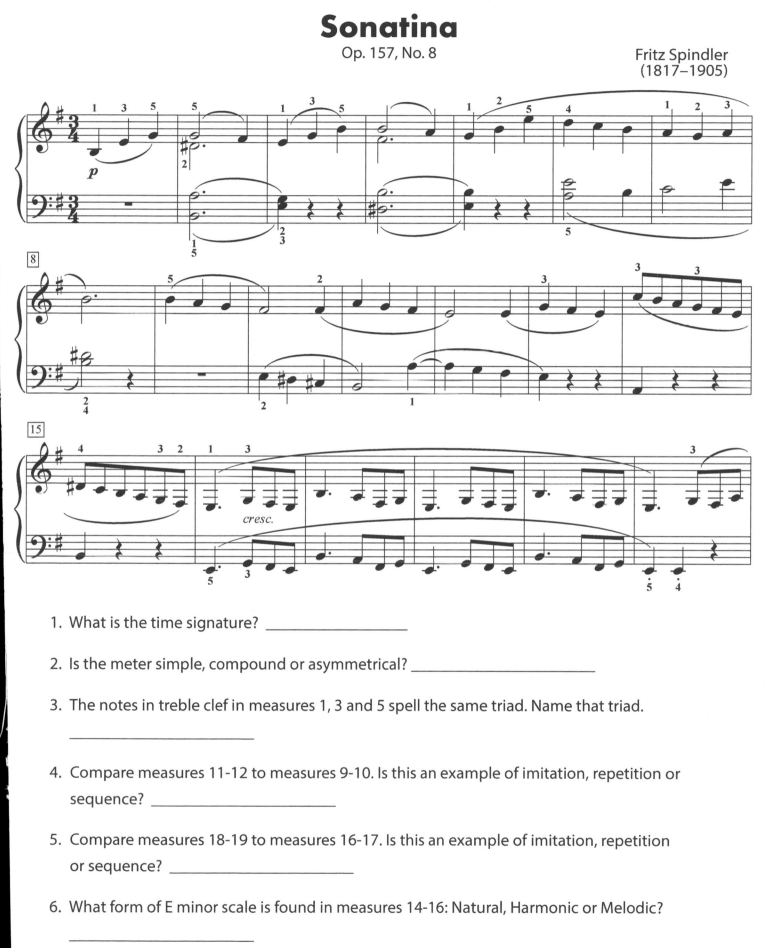

1. What is the time signature? _____

2. Is the meter simple, compound or asymmetrical? _____

3. The notes in treble clef in measures 1, 3 and 5 spell the same triad. Name that triad.

   _____

4. Compare measures 11-12 to measures 9-10. Is this an example of imitation, repetition or sequence? _____

5. Compare measures 18-19 to measures 16-17. Is this an example of imitation, repetition or sequence? _____

6. What form of E minor scale is found in measures 14-16: Natural, Harmonic or Melodic?

   _____

## Step Challenge

Starting at the bottom, work your way up the steps to find the answer.
Write your answer in the box.

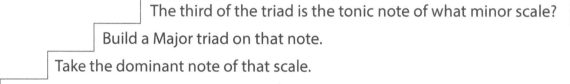

Name the key signature of that scale.

Build a minor scale on that note.

Take the 7th note of that scale.

1. Build a D Major scale.

The third of the triad is the tonic note of what minor scale?

Build a Major triad on that note.

Take the dominant note of that scale.

2. Build a c minor scale.

The 5th of the triad is what sharp in the order of sharps?

Build an Augmented triad on that note.

Go up a Perfect 5th.

3. Start with the note F.

Name that triad.

Build a Major triad.

Take the 6th note of that scale.

4. Build an f natural minor scale.

What note did you land on?

Go up a Major 3rd from that note.

Go up a Perfect 4th from that note.

5. Go up a minor 3rd from E♭.

# THEORY MASTERY

## Review Test

1. Draw bar lines where they are needed.

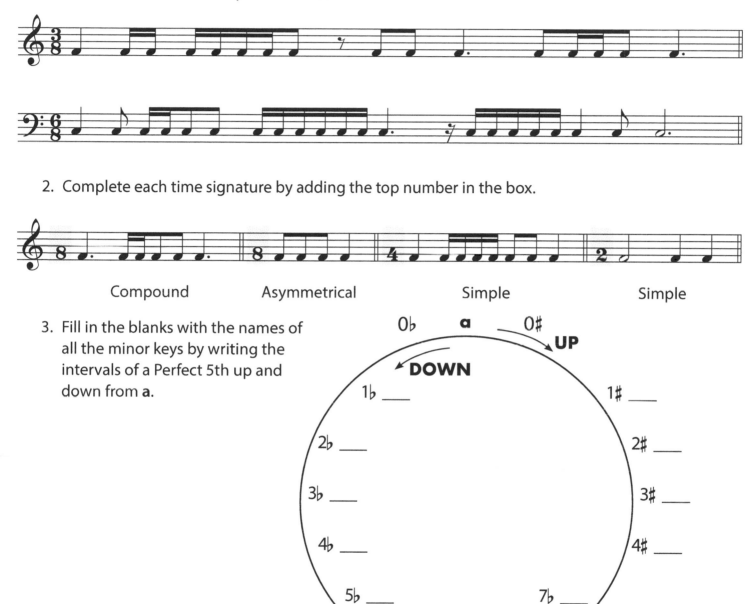

2. Complete each time signature by adding the top number in the box.

Compound      Asymmetrical      Simple      Simple

3. Fill in the blanks with the names of all the minor keys by writing the intervals of a Perfect 5th up and down from **a**.

4. Name the Major and relative minor keys. *The first one is done for you.*

G/e

5. Circle the correct name for each scale.

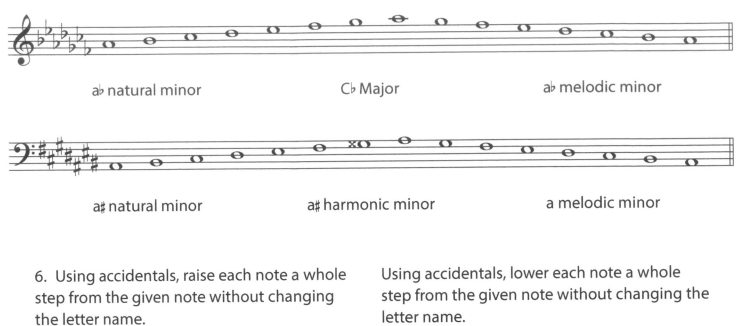

ab natural minor        Cb Major        ab melodic minor

a# natural minor        a# harmonic minor        a melodic minor

6. Using accidentals, raise each note a whole step from the given note without changing the letter name.

Using accidentals, lower each note a whole step from the given note without changing the letter name.

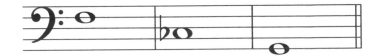

7. Complete the following sentences.

   a. To change Perfect or Major intervals to Augmented, _____ the upper note a half step.

   b. To change Perfect or minor intervals to diminished, _____ the upper note a half step.

   c. To change Major intervals to minor, _____ the upper note a half step.

8. Identify each interval by type and size.

_____  _____  _____  _____  _____

9.  Write the letter of the correct definition in the blank beside each term.

_____ imitation                    a. unison, 4ths, 5ths and 8ths of a Major scale

_____ Perfect intervals            b. beat can be divided by three

_____ meter                        c. Perfect interval decreased by a half step

_____ double sharp                 d. a melodic pattern restated in another voice

_____ diminished interval          e. 2nds, 3rds, 6ths and 7ths of a Major scale

_____ compound meter               f. lowers a flat note a half step

_____ simple meter                 g. the rhythmic structure of music

_____ Major intervals              h. beat can be divided by two

_____ enharmonic                   i. Perfect interval increased by a half step

_____ asymmetrical meter           j. a short, repeated melodic or rhythmic pattern

_____ double flat                  k. raises a sharp note a half step

_____ phrase                       l. combination of two simple meters, with an irregular pulse

_____ Augmented interval           m. more than one name for the same pitch

_____ minor interval               n. a musical thought or idea

_____ motive                       o. Major interval decreased by a half step

# Ear Training

1. You will hear four measures of rhythmic dictation. Fill in the blank measures with the rhythm you hear.

2. You will hear the following intervals played in broken and blocked form: M2, M3, P5, M6 and M7. Name the interval by type and size in each blank.

    1. _____    2. _____    3. _____    4. _____    5. _____    6. _____

3. You will hear melodic patterns using repetition or sequence. Circle the one you hear.

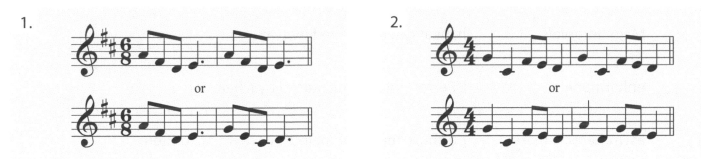

4. You will hear four scales ascending and descending. Circle the type of scale that you hear.

    a.  Major          natural minor          harmonic minor          melodic minor

    b.  Major          natural minor          harmonic minor          melodic minor

    c.  Major          natural minor          harmonic minor          melodic minor

    d.  Major          natural minor          harmonic minor          melodic minor